THINGS THAT MOVE

Devised and written by
Robin Wright

Designed and illustrated by
Teresa Foster

Edited by Tony Potter

Contents

About This Book

Whirligig

This book shows you how to make lots of things that move: jumping frogs, spinning whirligigs, bouncing bunnies and lots more.

All the different things you can make are shown here.

Mickey monkey

In the dog house

Every model is made from things you can find at home, like empty washing-up liquid bottles, elastic bands and corks. There is a list of things you need on each page.

Moving man dog show

Jumping frog

There are step-by-step instructions to follow and the patterns at the end of the book will help you to draw and cut out the difficult shapes.

You may need help from a grown-up for things marked with a sign like this:*

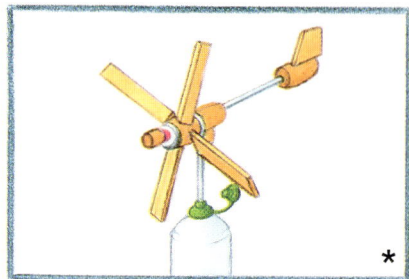

Peller vane

Drongo dragon

Jumping joey

Bouncing bunny game

About Things That Move

To make a ball move you have to hit, throw or kick it. It is your action that gives the ball the power to move.

But there are lots of ways to make things move. If you stretch a rubber band and let one end go it springs back.

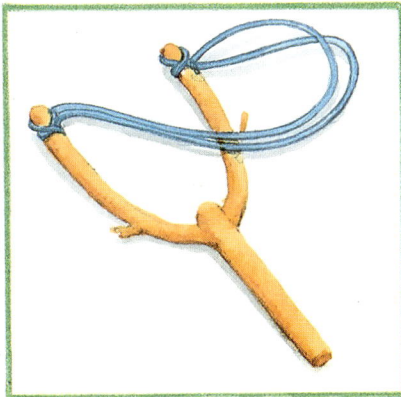

You can use this spring action as the power to make things jump, or shoot like a catapult.

If you twist a rubber band or a piece of string it will unwind itself and you can use this to make something turn or spin.

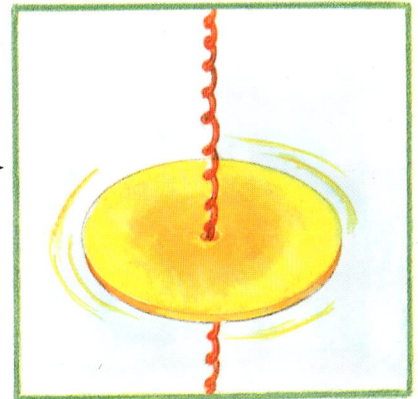

You can also make things turn or spin using the wind. A windmill begins to turn when the wind pushes against it. So, if you supply the power to push or pull an object you can make it move.
Power can come from a car engine, a simple twisted rubber band, or be as natural as the wind.

3

Making Things That Move

Read the instructions and the list of things you need first. Then get everything out before you start.

Cover the table with newspaper if you are going to use paint or glue.

Find an old wooden board to cut onto when you use the craft knife. Never cut onto the table itself.

Do not leave the craft knife or scissors where a baby can reach them. Put them away safely.

Use the patterns in the book and photocopy or trace the shapes you need to cut out. Cut them carefully.

Use just enough glue to hold things together. Too much makes everything sticky and takes longer to dry.

Put lids back on paint pots and glue as soon as you finish and wash out your paint brushes.

Put all your things away tidily and clear up any mess when you have finished working.

Let the paint and glue dry completely before you try out the things you have made.

Things You Need

You should be able to buy all these things from a craft or model shop, if you do not have them at home.

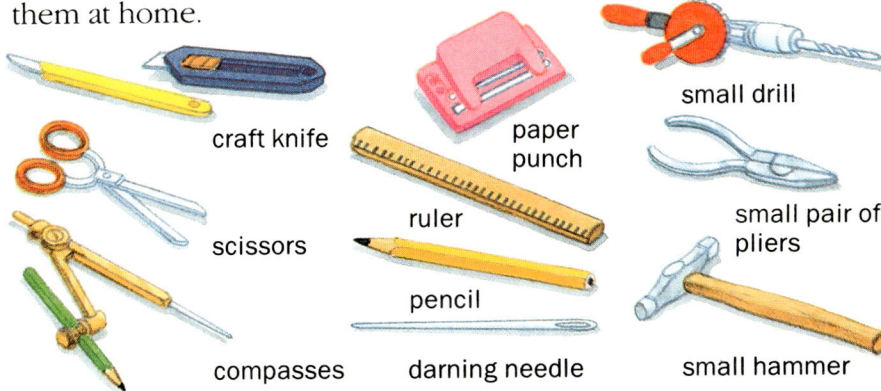

craft knife

scissors

compasses

paper punch

ruler

pencil

darning needle

small drill

small pair of pliers

small hammer

This page shows you all the tools and materials you need to make everything in this book.

Some things are more difficult to make than others so it is a good idea to ask a grown-up for help if you get stuck.

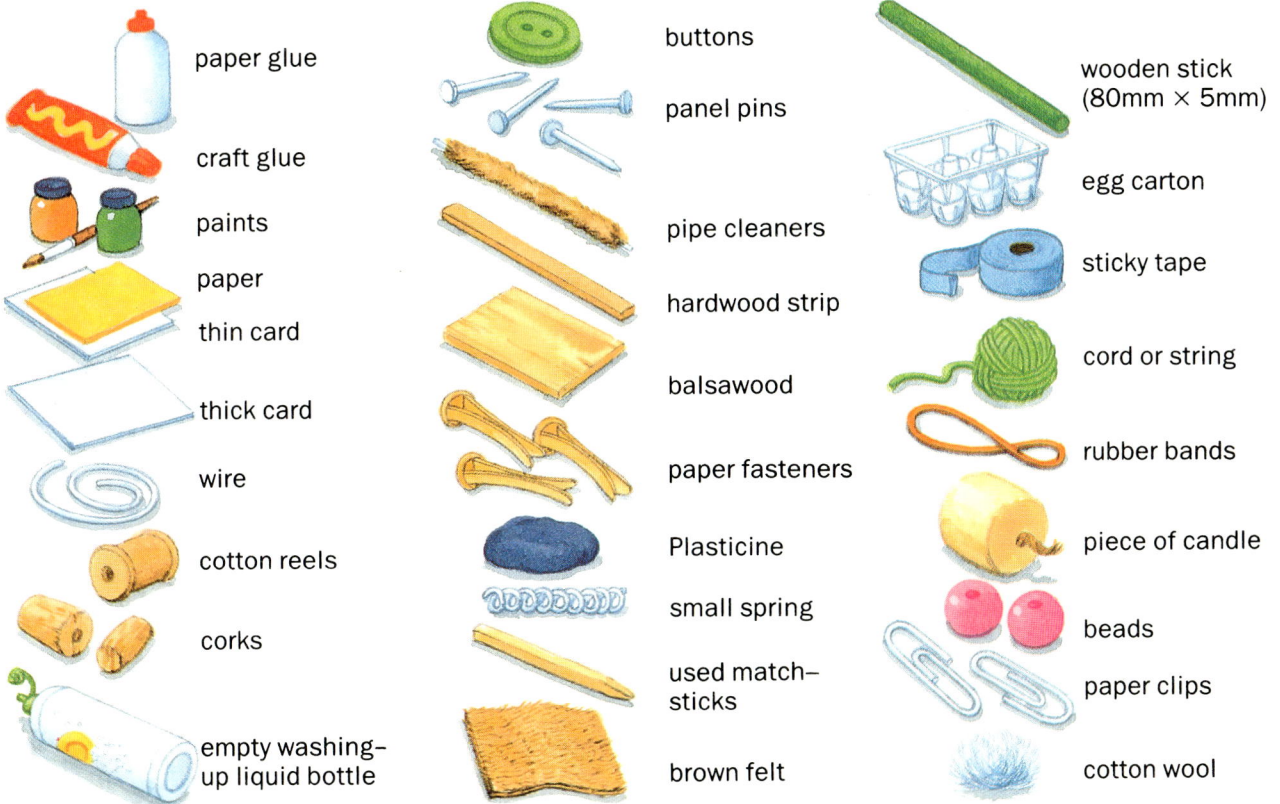

paper glue

craft glue

paints

paper

thin card

thick card

wire

cotton reels

corks

empty washing-up liquid bottle

buttons

panel pins

pipe cleaners

hardwood strip

balsawood

paper fasteners

Plasticine

small spring

used match-sticks

brown felt

wooden stick (80mm × 5mm)

egg carton

sticky tape

cord or string

rubber bands

piece of candle

beads

paper clips

cotton wool

Whirligig

Twist and pull the string to spin it,
Then you'll see the colours in it.
Yellow and red, or yellow and blue,
These colours make another two.

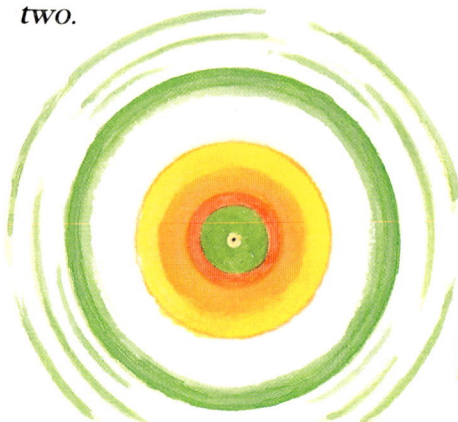

What you need

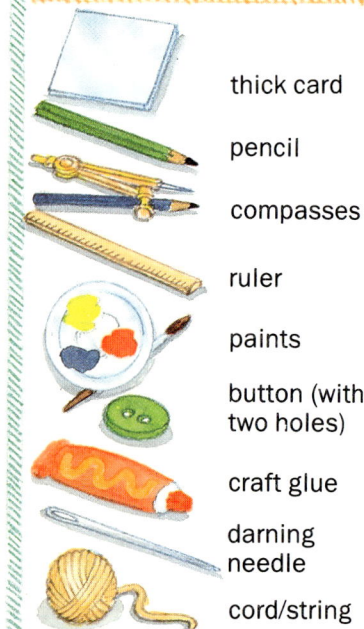

thick card

pencil

compasses

ruler

paints

button (with two holes)

craft glue

darning needle

cord/string

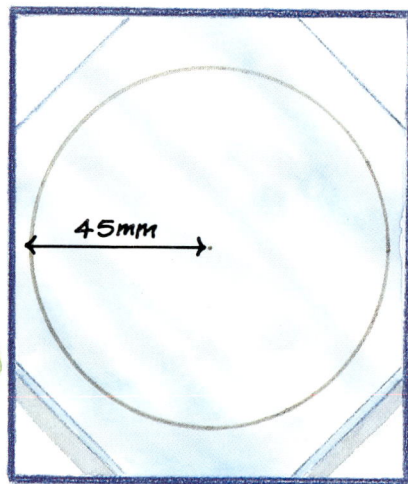

45mm

1 Set the points of your compasses 45mm apart and draw a circle on a piece of thick card.

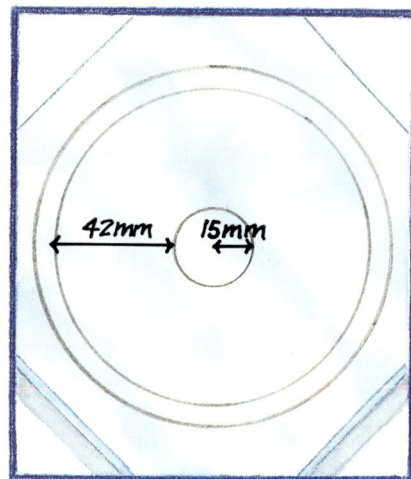

42mm 15mm

2 Draw two more circles inside the big one with your compasses set at 42mm and then at 15mm.

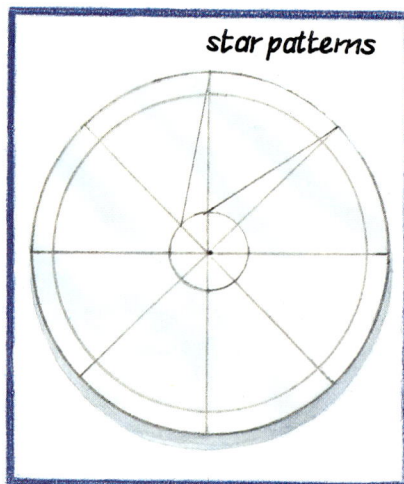

star patterns

3 Cut out the big circle and then with a pencil and ruler trace the star patterns onto each side.

4 Use the segments marked to paint red and yellow and blue and yellow patterns on both sides.

6 The patterns for this project are on page 24

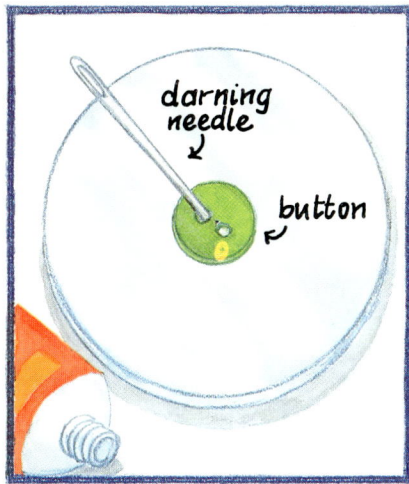

5 Glue the button exactly in the middle of one side. Make two holes in the card through the button's holes.

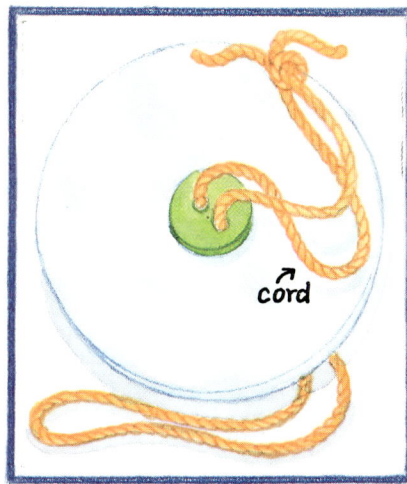

6 Thread a piece of cord or string through the two holes and tie the ends together firmly.

7 Put your fingers through the loops and twist up the string. Pull the string tight and it will untwist, spinning the whirligig. Loosen the string and it will twist up the other way. Repeat the action.

The string unwinds and spins the whirligig. The power of it spinning then makes the string twist up the other way.

As it turns the colours look as if they are mixed together. Yellow and blue make green; red and yellow make orange.

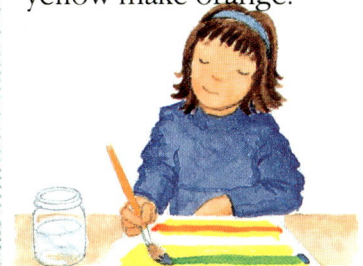

7

In The Dog House

*This mischievous pup keeps
running away,
But it's not safe to let her stray.
So spin the disk and then you'll see,
She'll return home, obediently.*

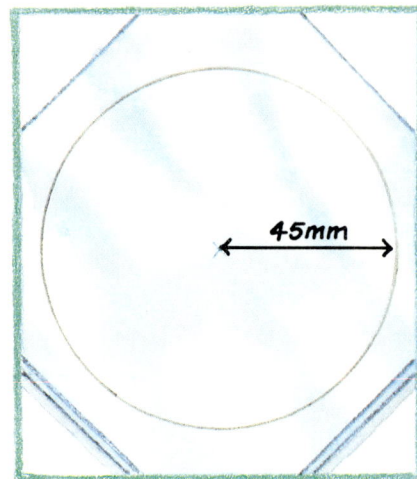

1 Set the points of your compasses 45mm apart and draw a circle on a piece of thick card.

What you need

 card

 paints

 compasses

 ruler

 pencil

 scissors

2 rubber bands

2 Cut out the circle. Trace the puppy on to one side using the pattern included and paint her.

The patterns for this project are on page 25

3 Turn the circle over and trace the kennel onto it so that it is the opposite way up to the puppy.

4 Make a hole each side of the circle. Thread a rubber band through each and fix as shown.

5 Hold and twist the rubber bands. As the circle spins the puppy will sit in the kennel.

Why it works

The twisted bands make the card spin. Because it spins fast, the picture of the puppy is still in your mind when you see the kennel picture. This makes it seem as if the puppy is inside her kennel.

Jumping Frog

mark fold line here

1 Trace the frog shape, two feet, two eyes and the spots onto thick card. Mark in the fold line.

2 Cut out all the pieces carefully.

What you need

thick card

rubber band

scissors

paper glue

pencil

ruler

paper punch

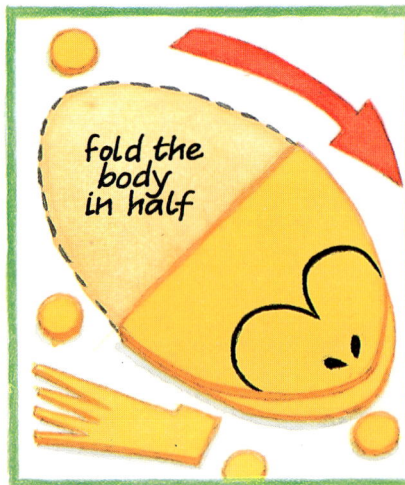

fold the body in half

3 Hold your scissors like a pencil and score along the fold line. Use a ruler edge to guide you.

feet
use a paper punch to make the holes

4 Glue the feet on the wrong side pointing away from the head. Make a hole each end of the body.

10 The patterns for this project are on page 26

5 Turn the frog over and paint in his face and body. Glue on the eyes and the spots.

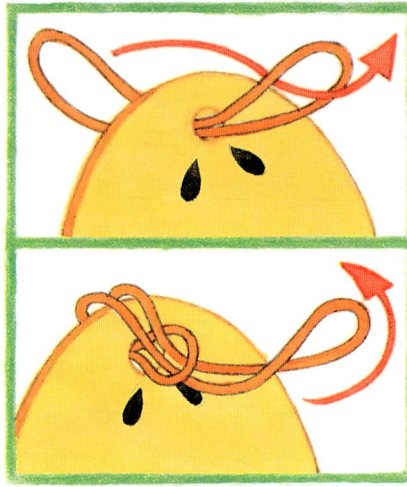

6 Thread a rubber band through one of the holes. Put one loop through the other and pull it tight.

7 Thread the rubber band through the other hole and make a knot in it to stop it slipping out.

8 Bend the frog inside out and then put him down. Watch him jump into the air.

Why it works

The rubber band stretches tight when the frog is inside out. Because the band is elastic, it springs back to its original length. This makes the frog's body flip back quickly so that it jumps.

Jumping Joey

egg pocket

tab ↗

1 Cut one egg pocket from the carton for the body. Leave a tab each side on the cut edge.

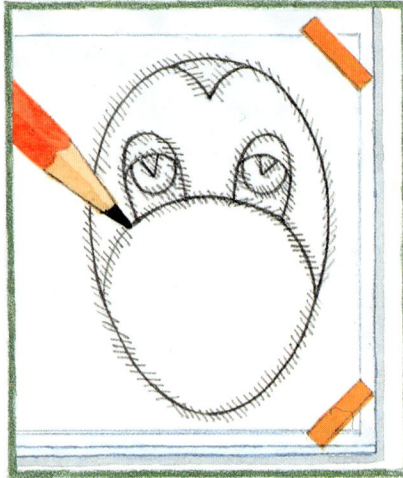

2 Trace the pattern pieces on to card and cut them all out.

top of egg pocket

3 Slice the top off one egg pocket for the nose. Glue it to the face. Paint or colour all the pieces.

What you need

egg carton

card
felt

7mm spring
20mm long

cork

craft knife

craft glue

paints
felt-tip pens

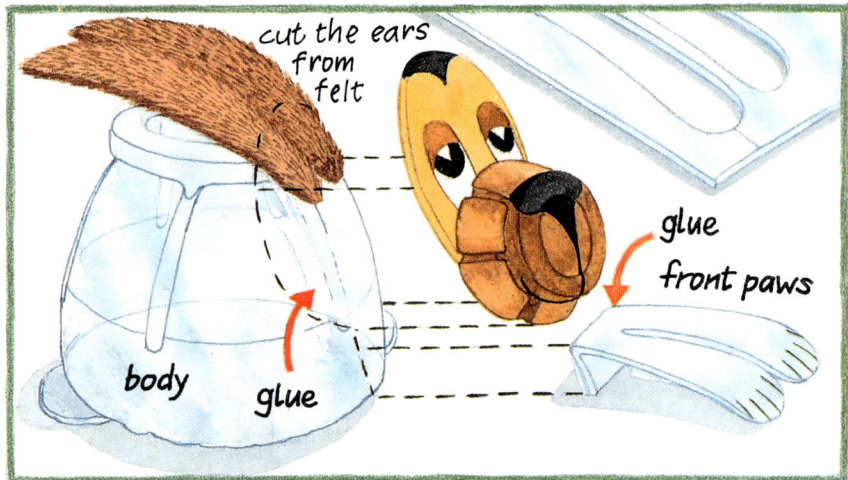

cut the ears from felt

glue front paws

body   glue

4 Glue the ears to the body and then stick on the face. Stick the front paws on the body under the chin.

The patterns for this project are on page 27

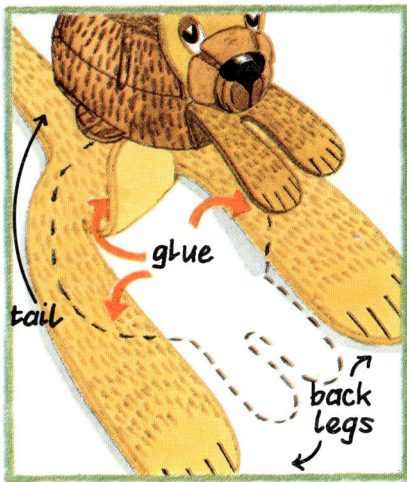

5   Glue the body onto the back legs and tail piece. When it is dry bend the tail up slightly.

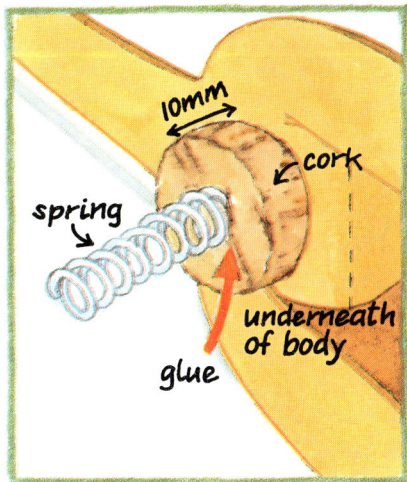

tail

glue

back legs

6   Cut a 10mm round of cork. Make a hole and glue the spring into it. Glue the cork under the body.

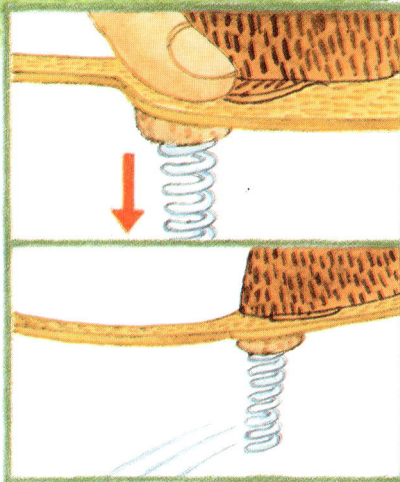

10mm

cork

spring

underneath of body

glue

7   Stand Joey on his spring. Press him down each side of his tail. When you let go he will jump up.

Why it works

As you press down with your fingers, the spring squeezes up. When you let go the spring jumps back to its original length. This pushes Joey upwards and makes him jump.

Drongo Dragon

*Drongo's a dragon it's quite
plain to see.
With that fiery snout,
What else could he be?*

What you need

paper

pencil

scissors

glue

paints

cotton reel

piece of
candle

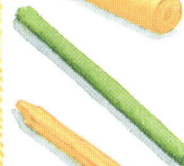
5mm wooden
stick, 80mm
long

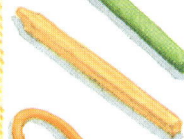
used
  matchstick

rubber band

craft knife

sticky tape

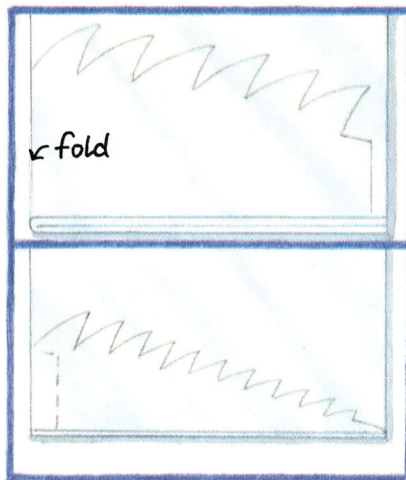

1 Fold paper in two. Trace
body pattern with front edge
on fold. Trace other pieces
onto single paper.

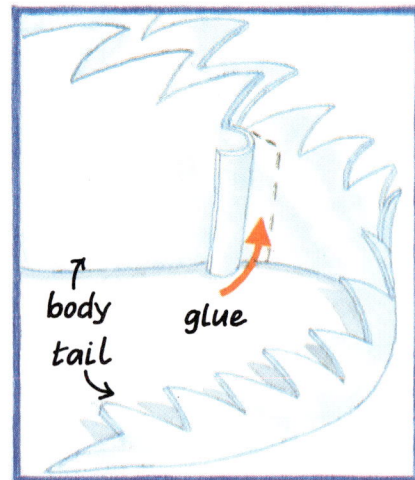

2 Cut out all the pieces.
Glue the tail between the two
ends of the body. Paint the
body and tail.

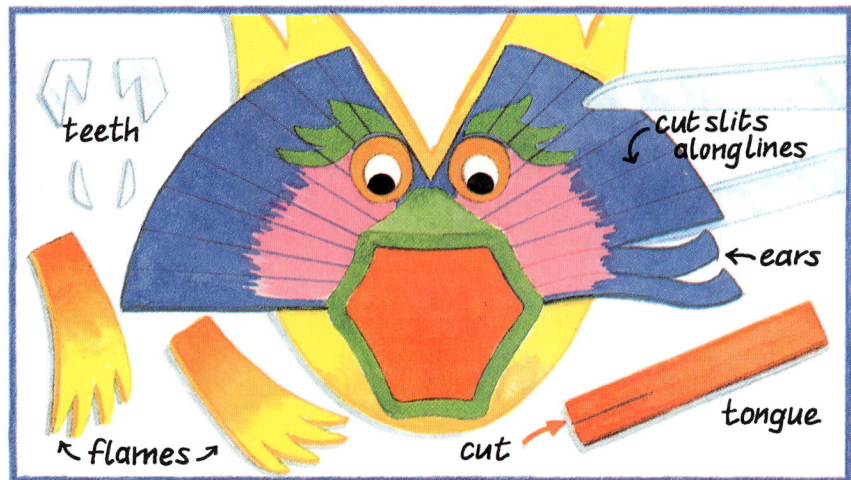

3 Paint the teeth, flames,
tongue and face pieces. When
the paint is dry, cut slits in the
ears to make them curl and
make the cut marked on the
tongue. Glue on his teeth,
tongue and flames.

4 Cut a 15mm slice from the end of a candle. Make a hole through it using the point of a scissor blade.

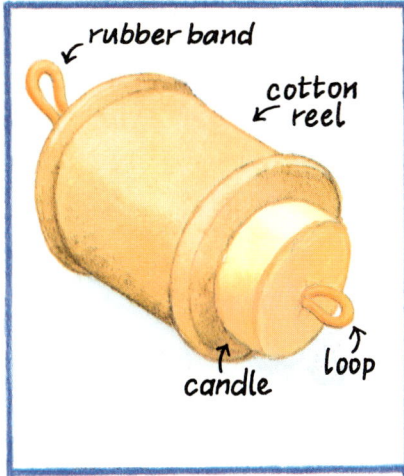

rubber band

cotton reel

candle

loop

5 Thread the rubber band through the cotton reel and the piece of candle so there is a loop each end.

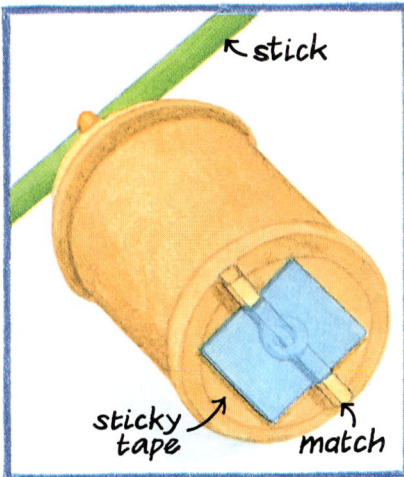

↖stick

motor goes here ↓

stick

cotton reel motor ↙

look at the big picture of Drongo to see where the motor goes

sticky tape

match

6 Put the stick through one loop and the match through the other. Tape the match so it will not move.

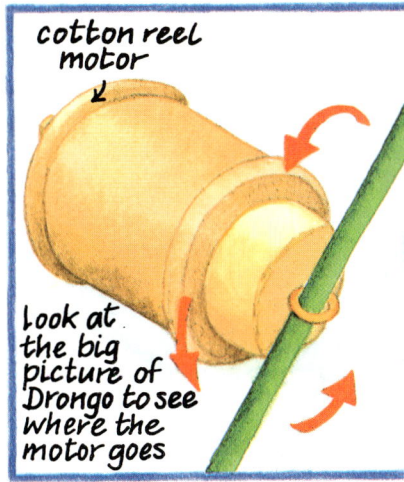

7 Turn the stick to wind up the rubber band. Put the cotton reel in Drongo's body behind his head.

Why it works

The rubber band unwinds, turning the stick. The stick acts as a lever and makes the cotton reel roll along. It pushes against Drongo's head and makes him move forward.

15

Bouncing Bunny Game

The Bouncing Bunnies will soon get wise,
And want that juicy carrot prize.
They'll jump up high so they can eat
This, their favourite bunny treat!

What you need

egg carton

craft knife

scissors

card

green paper

felt

cotton wool

paints

felt-tip pens

craft glue

Plasticine
2 corks
3 balsawood boards
50mm × 100mm × 5mm thick
sticky tape
rubber band

1 Cut one egg pocket from the carton to make the body. Paint or colour it with felt tip pens.

2 Trace the feet and face shapes onto card and the ears on felt. Cut them out and colour the card pieces.

3 Slice the top off one egg pocket to make the nose. Colour it then glue it onto the face.

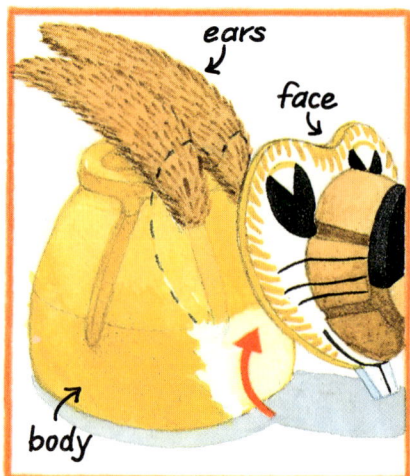

4 Glue the ears onto the body and then stick the face in position over them.

16 The patterns for this project are on page 29

How to play

Hold the balsawood boards flat. Sit your Bunny on one end. Let that end go and it will flip Bunny up. The object of the game is to aim your Bunny as close to the carrot target as possible.

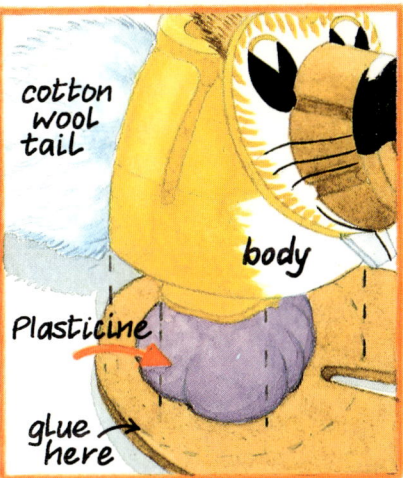

cotton wool tail

body

Plasticine

glue here

5 Stick a Plasticine weight on the feet. Glue the body on over it. Add a cotton wool tail.

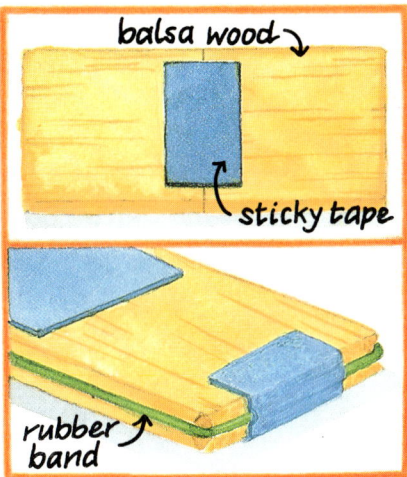

Why it works

When you press the boards down flat, the rubber band stretches. When you let one end go, the band springs back to its original length flipping one board up. This movement shoots Bunny up into the air.

balsa wood

sticky tape

rubber band

6 Tape two balsawood boards together. Stretch a rubber band round the edge and tape it on each end.

leaves made from paper

carrot target

balsa wood base

7 Make a carrot from coloured cork and green paper. Glue it on to a balsawood stand.

17

Moving Man Dog Show

This young hound just loves to play,
You push, he pulls the other way;
The hidden lever is the clue
To the tug-o-war between these two.

What you need

 thick card

 4 paper fasteners

 felt

 craft glue

 pencil

 scissors

 felt-tip pens

 craft knife

make the holes with a paper punch or something pointed

1 Trace the man's body and arm and the dog's head and body onto thick card. Mark all the holes for the paper fasteners carefully. Cut out the shapes and colour them in on one side.

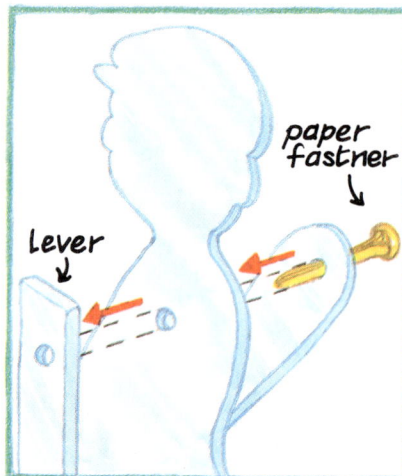

lever

paper fastner

2 Cut a card strip 270mm × 10mm for the lever. Fix it and the arm to the body with a paper fastener.

grass made from a long card strip

lever →

paper fastener

3 Cut a card strip 220mm × 30mm. Colour in the grass. Fix the foot, grass and lever with a paper fastener.

18 The patterns for this project are on page 30

tail

felt

glue

ear

teeth

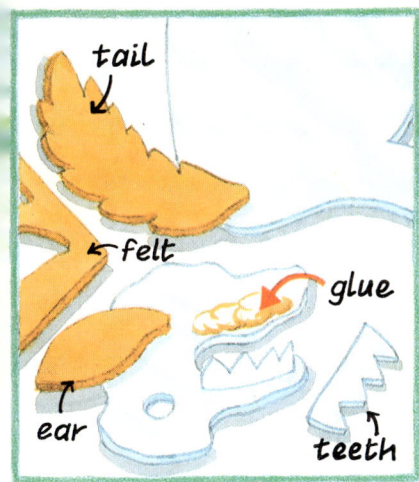

4 Trace the dog's ears and tail onto felt. Cut them out. Make the teeth out of paper. Glue them in place.

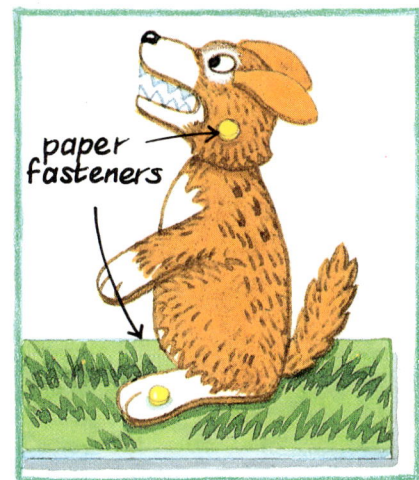

paper fasteners

5 Use paper fasteners to fix the dog's head to its body and its foot to the grass strip.

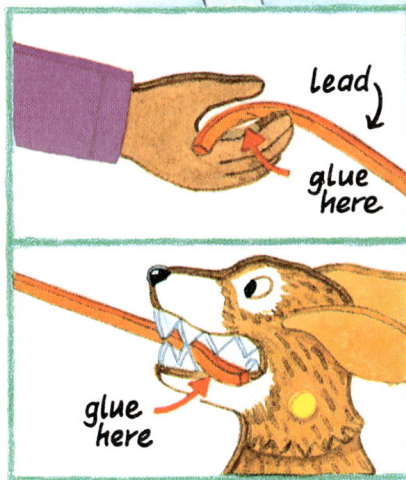

lead

glue here

glue here

6 Cut a lead out of card. Colour it and glue one end in the dog's mouth and the other in the man's hand.

Why it works

The card strip that goes from the man's arm and through his foot is a lever. When you move the lever it pushes the arm and the lead making the dog move. The joints made with paper fasteners make this movement possible.

Peller Vane

The Peller Vane spins when the wind blows,
The stronger the wind, the faster it goes.

What you need

1 big cork with a hole in it

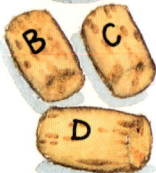

3 smaller corks

2mm wire 540mm long

balsawood, 120mm × 120mm × 5mm thick

2 wooden beads

thick card

craft glue

craft knife

small pair of pliers

pencil

ruler

empty washing-up liquid bottle

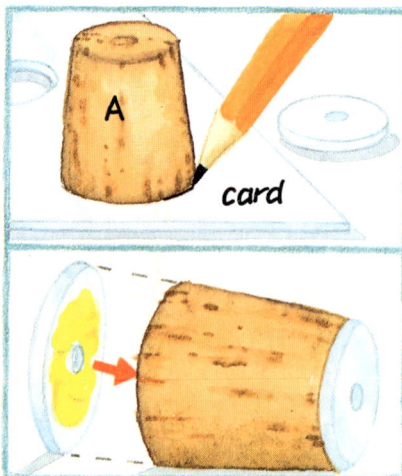

1 Cut two card circles the same size as the big cork A. Make holes in the middle of each and glue them on.

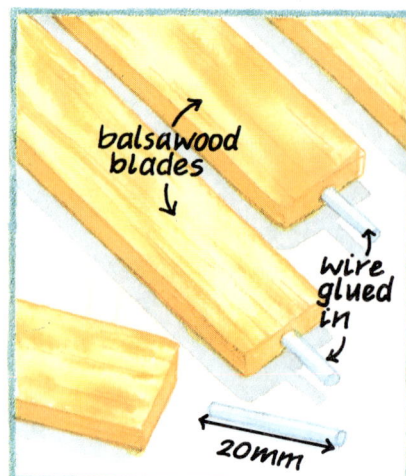

2 Cut four balsawood blades 120mm × 20mm. Push and glue a 20mm wire in the middle of one end of each.

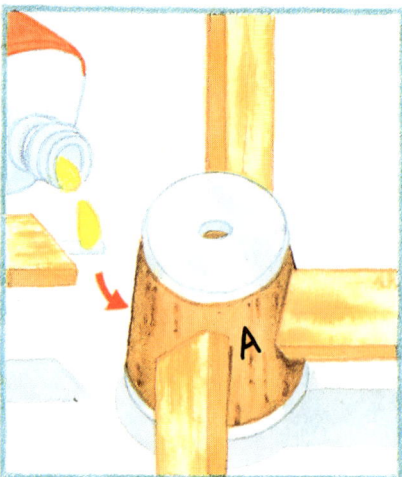

balsawood blades

wire glued in

20mm

3 Make four equally spaced holes in cork A. Push in the wires and glue the blades at a slight angle.

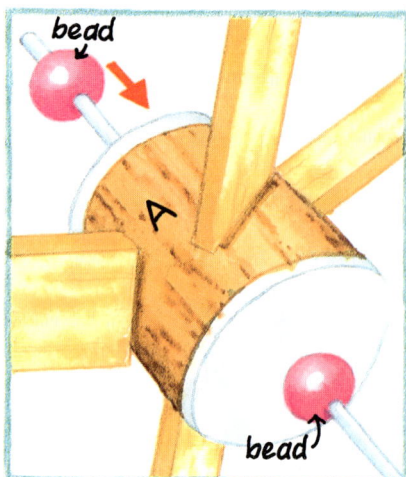

4 Cut 180mm of wire. Push it through cork A so 20mm shows one end. Slide the beads on from each end.

bead

bead

20 The patterns for this project are on page 29

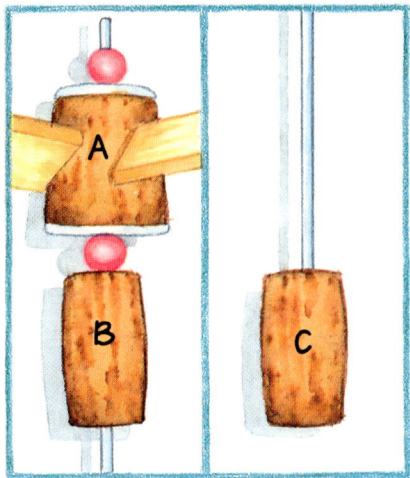

5 Slide cork B up the long wire to the bead. Push and glue cork C onto the tail end of the long wire.

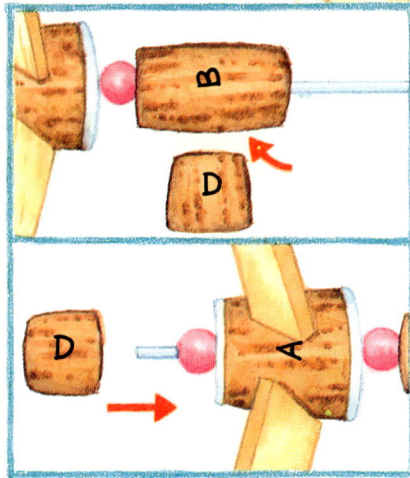

6 Cut cork D in half. Glue one half to cork B. Push and glue the other half on the short end of wire.

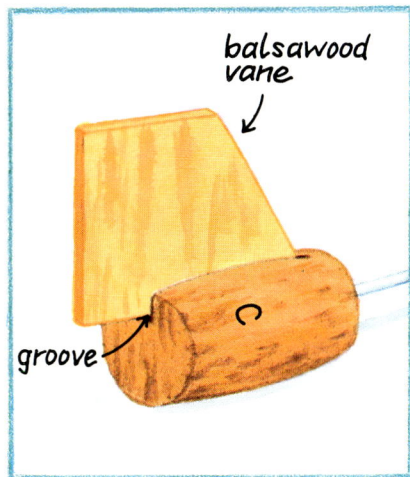

balsawood vane

groove

C

7 Cut a balsawood vane using the pattern. Make a groove in tail cork C and glue the vane in place.

you may need to fill the washing-up liquid bottle with water to stop the Peller Vane falling over

D

8 Glue the remaining wire into the half cork D below cork B. Stand the end in a washing-up liquid bottle.

Why it works

The wind blows against the blades. The blades are angled so that when the wind pushes on them they start to turn.

The wind vane on cork C keeps the blades facing into the wind even if it changes and blows from another direction.

Mickey Monkey

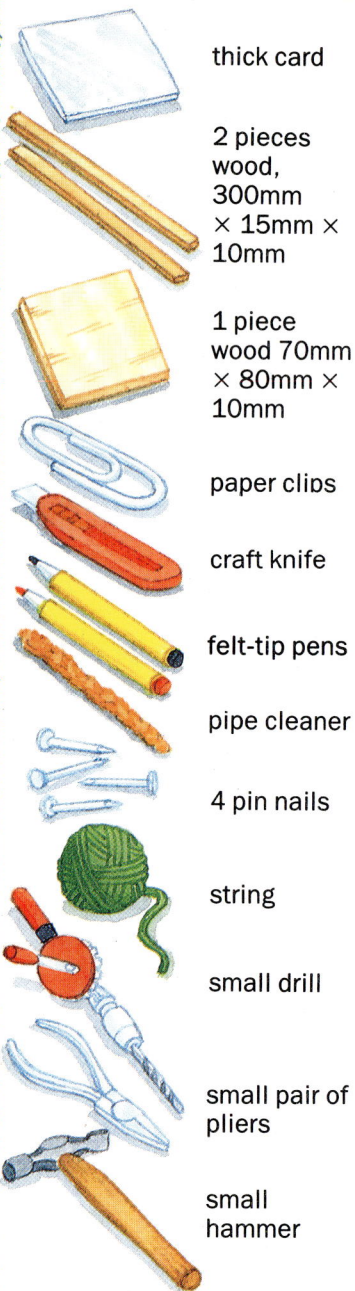

1 Trace the shapes for the body, two arms and two legs and hand-spacers onto card. Colour and cut them out.

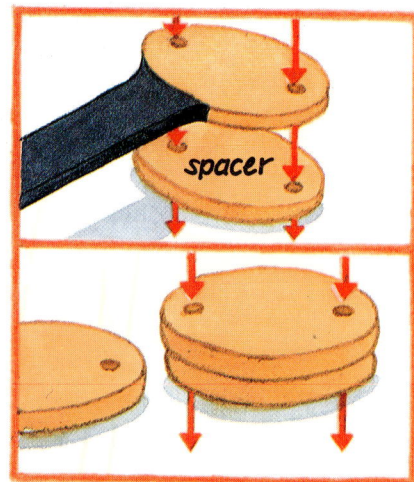

hand spacers

2 Make two holes as marked through the hands and hand-spacers with a nail. Make sure the holes are all in line.

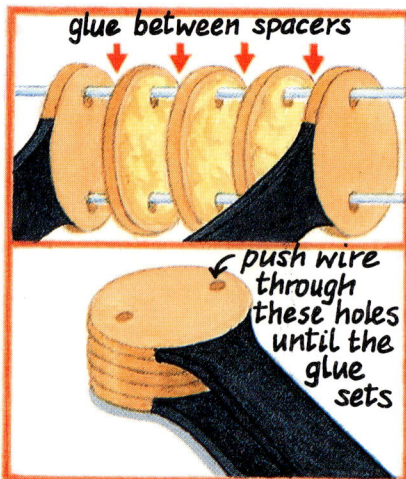

spacer

3 Glue them together and push some wire through the holes to keep them open. Then remove wire.

glue between spacers

push wire through these holes until the glue sets

4 Use paper clip wire, bent over to attach the arms and legs to the body. Add a pipe cleaner tail.

bent paper clip

bent paper clip

make a hole and glue in the tail

The pattern for this project is on page 31

get someone to hold the wood while you drill the holes

drill wood

use scrap wood to drill into

5 Drill two holes at the top of each of the long pieces of wood.

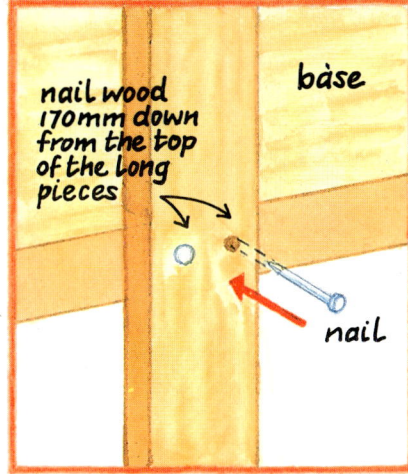

nail wood 170mm down from the top of the long pieces

base

nail

6 Nail the other piece of wood between the two long pieces halfway down them.

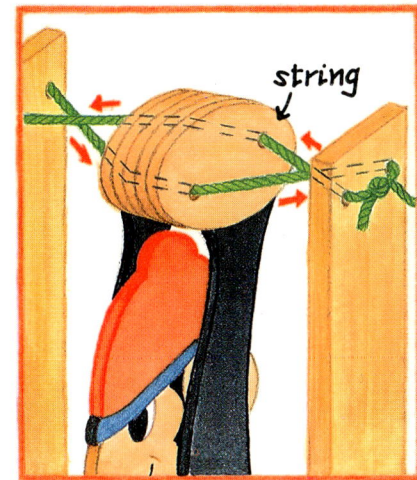

string

7 Thread the string as shown through the holes in the wood and the monkey's hands. Tie the ends together.

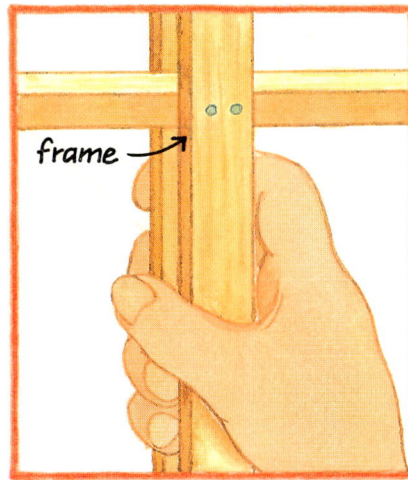

frame

8 Hold the frame and squeeze the ends together to make the monkey somersault.

How it works

By squeezing the strips you stretch the string. This untwists it, making Mickie somersault. As he does so, he makes the string twist again.

23

Patterns

Whirligig

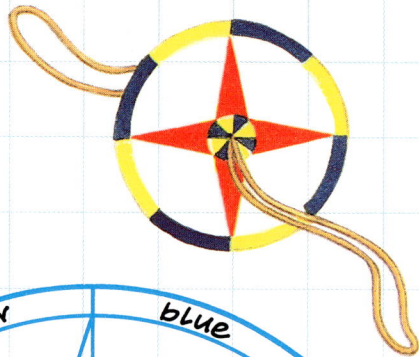

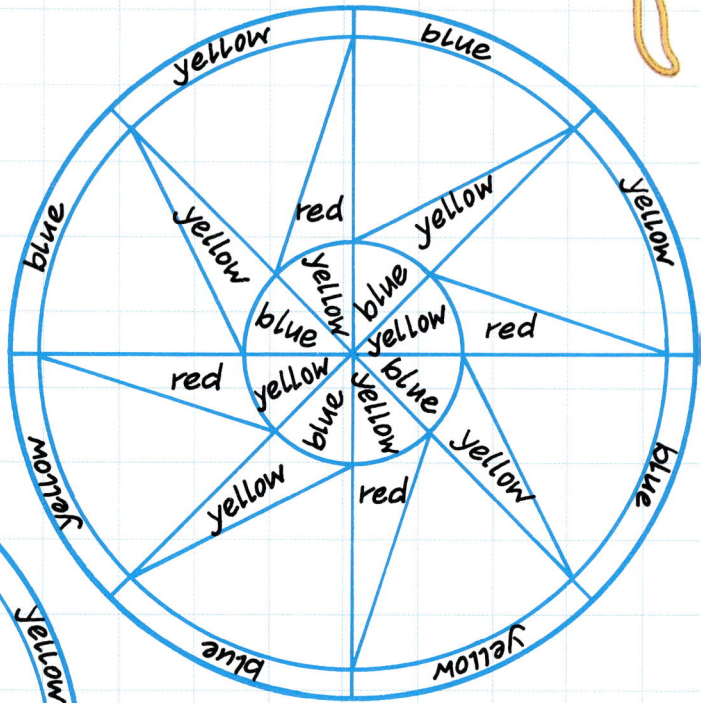

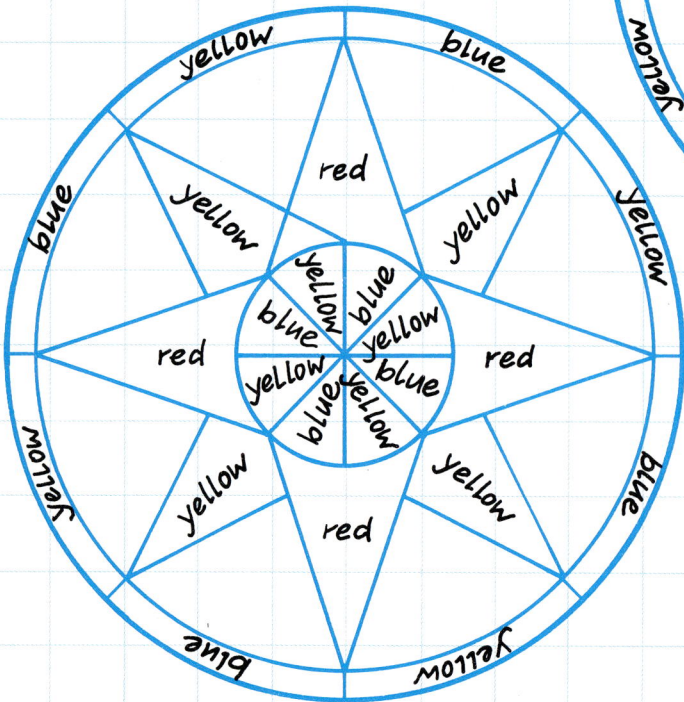

In The Dog House

Jumping Frog

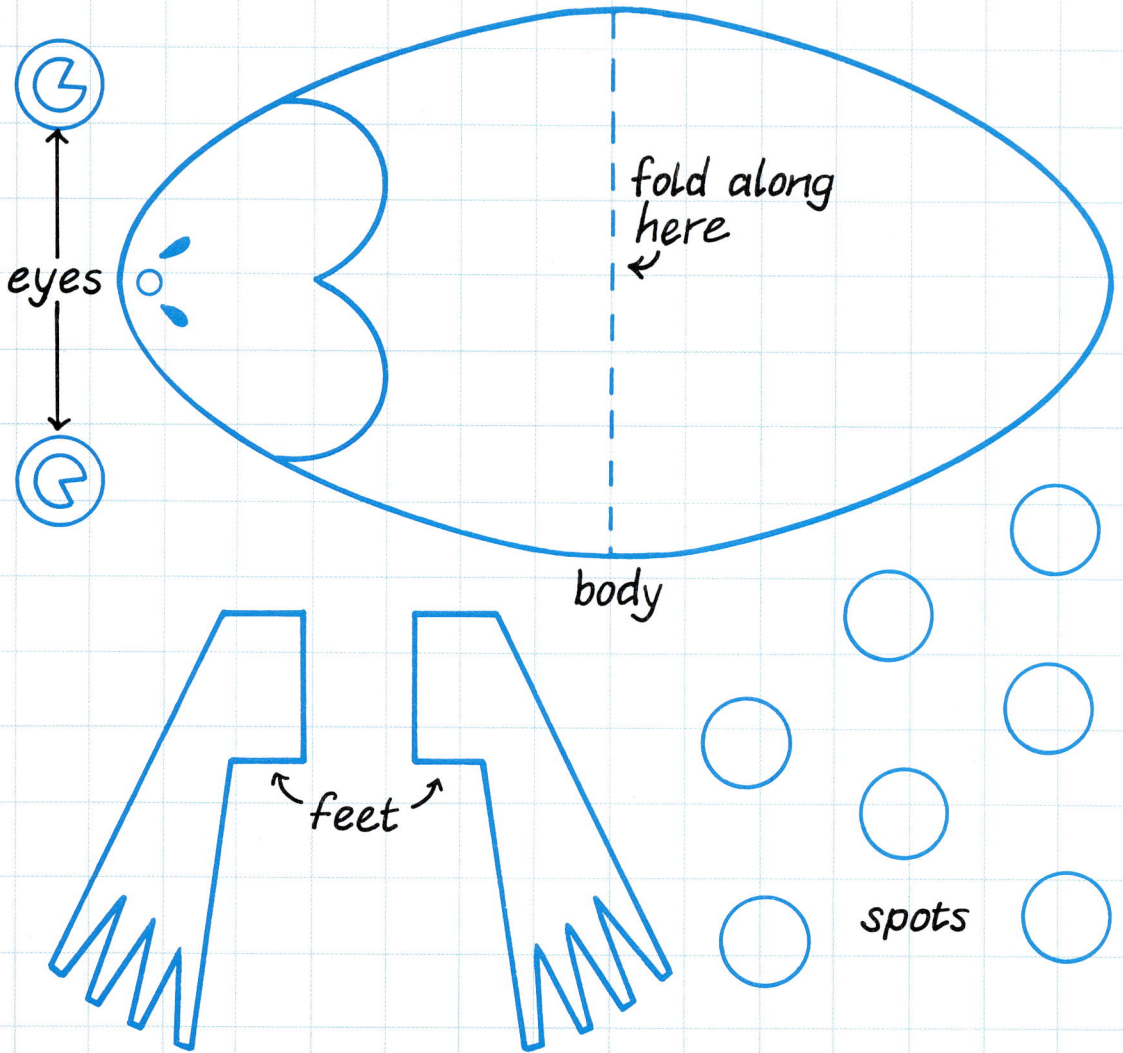

eyes

fold along here

body

feet

spots

Jumping Joey

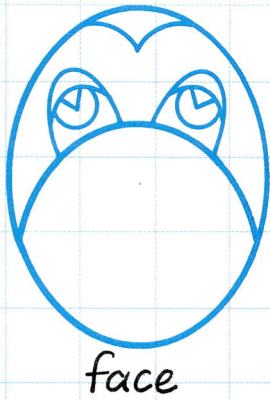

face

feet

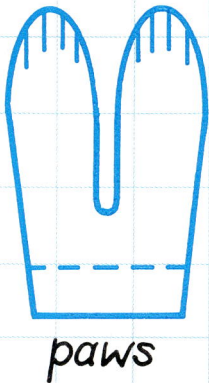

paws

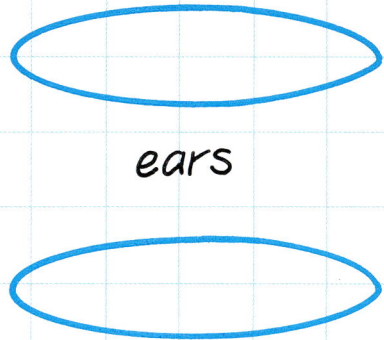

ears

Drongo Dragon

body

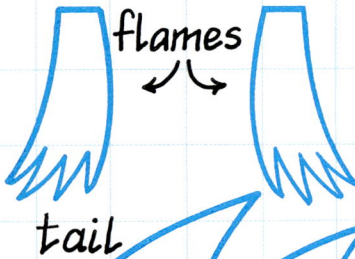

flames

tail

tongue

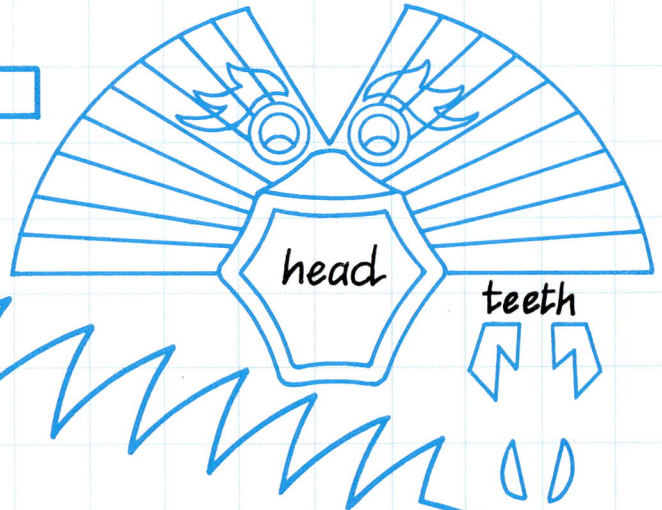

head

teeth

Bouncing Bunny

back legs

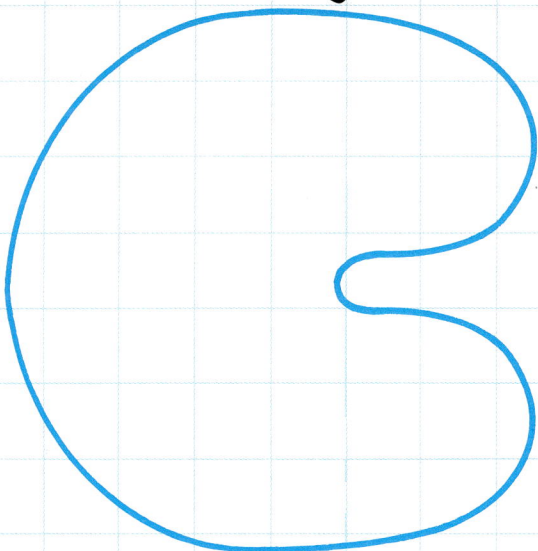

ears

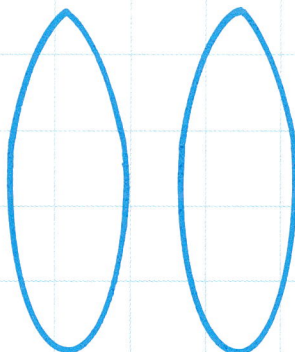

face

Peller Vane

blade

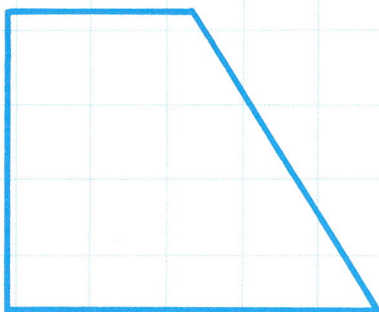

vane

29

Moving Man Dog Show

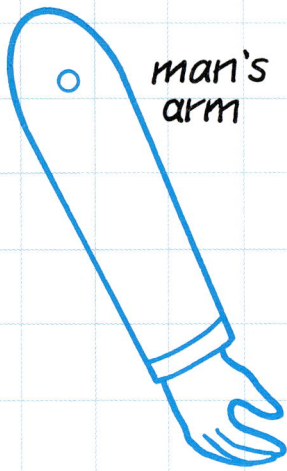

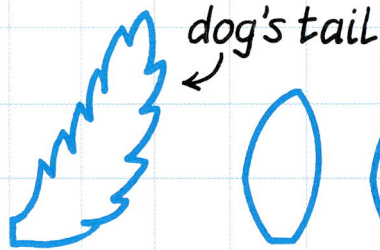

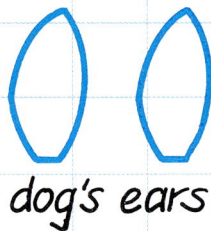

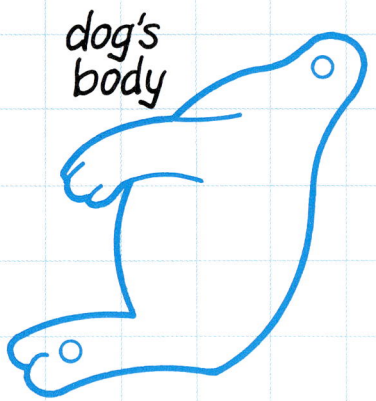

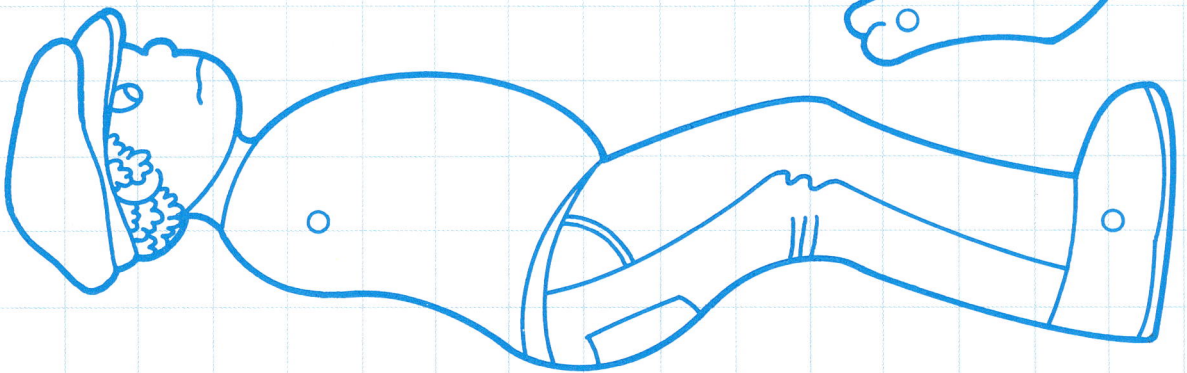

man's arm

dog's teeth

dog's tail

dog's ears

dog's head

dog's body

Mickey Monkey

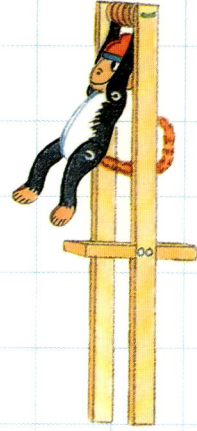

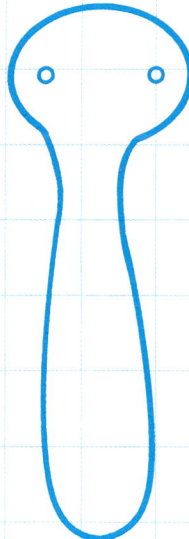

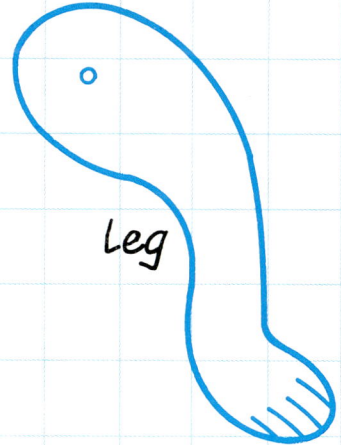

base

arm

Leg

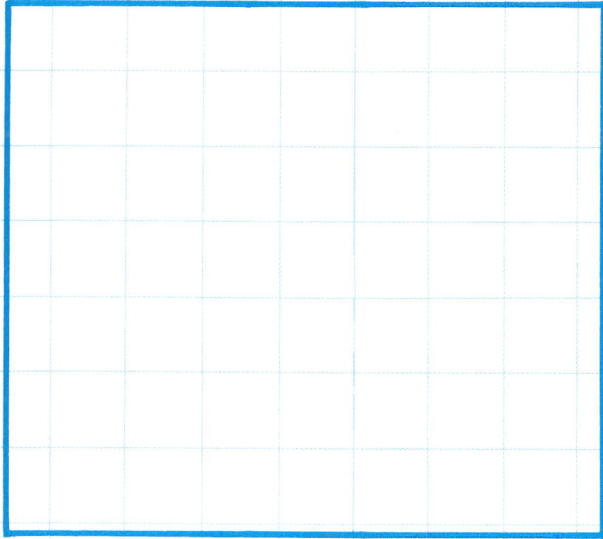

body

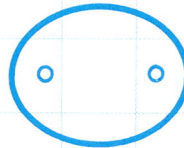

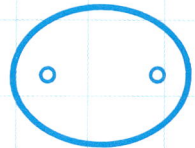

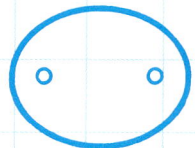

spacers

William Collins Sons & Co Ltd
London · Glasgow · Sydney · Auckland
Toronto · Johannesburg
First published 1989
© William Collins Sons & Co Ltd 1989

A CIP catalogue record for this book is
available from the British Library

ISBN 0 00 190030-7 Hardback
      0 00 190062-5 Paperback
All rights reserved

Printed in Portugal by Resopal